Shady Bay
ARCHIE GOES TO THE DOCTOR

Created by Emma Brown

This is Archie and his sister, Amber.
They live in Shady Bay.

Archie and Amber love to play outside.
"Let's play hide and seek," says Archie.
"It's your turn to hide."

"1, 2, 3, 4, 5…," counts Archie.

Next Archie plays on the swing. Amber reads her book. "Watch me!" says Archie.

Archie stands on the swing.
He swings higher and higher…

…and then, whoops! He slips and falls.
"Ouch! I've hurt my arm. Fetch
Mummy!" Archie cries.

"I'm going to take you
to the doctor," says Mummy.

"Don't worry," says Amber.
"Dr Hodge is very kind.
He will soon make you
feel better."

While Mummy phones the doctor,
Amber reads Archie a story.

"I can't turn the pages,"
says Archie. "My arm hurts."

"Let's take your doctor's play set with us. Bunny can come too," says Amber.

"Can you carry them? My arm hurts," says Archie.

In the doctor's waiting
room there is a fish tank.

"How many fish can you see,
Archie?" asks Amber.
"Five," says Archie.

Archie's friend, Breeze, comes into
the waiting room with her Daddy.

"What's wrong, Breeze?" asks Archie.

"My ears hurt," she says.

They watch Amber do a jigsaw.
"Do you want to help me?" asks Amber.

"I can't," says Archie.
"My arm hurts."

It is Archie's turn to see the doctor.

"Hello, I'm Dr Hodge," says the doctor.
"What have you done, Archie?"

"I fell off the swing," says
Archie. "My arm hurts."

Dr Hodge looks at Archie's arm.

"No broken bones!" he says.
"We'll soon make you feel better."

"That's a relief," says Mummy.

The doctor puts a sling on Archie's arm.

Archie begins to
feel a bit better.

"You can go home now,"
says Dr Hodge, "but no
running around!"

Archie sits next to Breeze in the waiting room.

"Look at my sling," he says. "Dr Hodge is very nice. He will make you feel better soon."

At home, Archie has ice-cream for being brave.

Amber has an
ice lolly for being
so kind and helpful.

A few days later, Archie and Breeze are both feeling better. Breeze comes round to Archie's house.

"Let's play doctors," says Archie.

Breeze looks in Archie's ears.

Archie puts a sling on Breeze's arm.

Archie and Breeze go outside.
Breeze gets on the swing.

"Don't fall, Breeze!" says Archie.